He Walks With Me

He Walks With Me

Susan R. Lawrence

Gannah Group Publications

He Walks With Me

ISBN: 978-1-946985-15-6

©2024 Gannah Group Publications

All rights reserved. Non-commercial interested parties may reproduce portions of this book without the express written permission of the publisher, provided the text does not exceed 500 words.

Commercial interests: No part of this publication may be reproduced in any form, stored in a retrieval system, or transmitted in any form by any means—electronic, photocopy, recording, or otherwise—without prior written permission of the publisher.

Scripture quotations are from the Holy Bible, New International Version (2005).

Cover design
by Lynn Edler
LE Design

Dedication

To my four friends who have hiked many miles with me—Leigh, Angela, Gwen, and Maggie. Let's go for a walk in the woods!

Acknowledgements

Publishing has often been referred to as "birthing a book," and this is an apt reference. I would not have wanted to give birth to my two sons without all the nurses, doctors, and my husband to attend. And I am grateful for all those who attended the birth of *He Walks With Me*.

Thank you to my editor, Gwen, of Illuminate Editing and also to my two critique groups, Des Moines Word Weavers and Sharpened Pencils—all of your suggestions polished my work to perfection. Thank you to my publisher, Gannah Group Publications. You have done a stellar job, as always.

And thank you to my friends and family, especially my husband, Gary. You are my cheerleaders, and I might have stopped writing long ago without your encouragement.

Thanks always to God the Father and to my Savior, Jesus Christ, for walking with me, not only on my writing journey, but guiding my life every moment of every day. To God be the Glory!

The Yolk

Come to me, all you who are weary and burdened, and I will give you rest. Take my yoke upon you and learn from me, for I am gentle and humble in heart, and you will find rest for your souls. For my yoke is easy and my burden is light. (Matthew 11:28-30)

When I ask my two-year-old Labrador retriever, "Want to go for a walk?" she becomes a leaping, wiggling bundle of joy. I hold out the leash and the prong collar, a restraint that gently pokes her if she pulls too hard. Maggie doesn't turn away, she comes and slips her head willingly into the collar. She knows the only way a walk will happen is when she is harnessed to me. Then we can explore the wooded trails she loves.

When we say to Jesus, "I believe in You and trust you for my salvation," we begin a walk with Him. Much as I hold the collar for my pup, Jesus holds out an invisible harness for us. We can anticipate delightful, shaded paths and rest for our souls if we slip into the yoke and stay connected to our Lord. He may lead us also onto rocky, difficult paths, but He will remain yoked with us. Occasionally the collar may restrain, or poke us, or even lead us a different direction than we are headed, but being harnessed with the One who loves and knows us best will ultimately bring us peace and joy.

Susan R. Lawrence

Conversing With My Guide
Lord Jesus, may I accept your yoke with joy, knowing it is the only way I can go on the paths you have prepared for me.

Climbing Higher
Read 1 John 1-3

Stepping Out in Faith
Place a bracelet, rubber band, or string around your wrist for a day. Picture yourself in a harness with Jesus. Use the bracelet to remind you to thank Him for the opportunity to walk with Him, learn from Him, and have rest for your soul.

Trail Notes (questions, insights, prayers)

_____

_____

_____

_____

_____

_____

Backpacks

Cast your cares on the Lord and He will sustain you; he will never let the righteous fall. (Psalm 55:22)

One of the first and most important items on a hiker's list is the backpack. I chose mine carefully—making sure it fit comfortably, had all the right pockets, and didn't weigh too much. And, of course, I chose an attractive aqua color. Then I added all the necessary items: water, first aid kit, cooling towel, phone, extra camera, guidebook, maps, my lunch and snacks, food and collapsible dish for my dog, Maggie, extra socks, a flashlight, a safety whistle, a journal, water purification system, and, wow! my pack got heavy. And I had none of the essentials a through-hiker would carry such as a tent, sleeping bag, and cooking utensils.

I looked over my pack's contents again, sorting what I was certain was necessary and what could be unloaded. At last, I hefted my much lighter pack onto my back and strapped it on. I no longer carried weight I didn't need.

Walking through life, we carry backpacks, too. When we are children, they are relatively light. Maybe a worry or two about who will be your friend or your score on a spelling test. These concerns are quickly discarded within days.

But as we grow, we load our packs with weightier items—career choices, marriage, and children. We jam things in tightly as our families grow and our teenagers begin to navigate their way in the world, adding their worries to our own. By the time we have grandchildren, these backpacks can become monstrous burdens. But we still stubbornly attempt to carry them.

Our loving God does not intend for us carry these burdens. He is the Sustainer who will provide for our needs and the needs of our loved ones. Empty those backpacks into His caring arms and you will hike higher and farther than ever before.

Conversing With My Guide
Jesus, the burdens I carry wear me down. I am exhausted in body and soul. Help me to release my anxieties to you and trust in your perfect peace.

Climbing Higher
1 Peter 5:7
Psalm 68:19
Isaiah 26:3
Matthew 6:34

Stepping Out in Faith
Make a list of the items in your backpack—the worries and anxieties you are trying to carry yourself. Pray over each one, releasing them to the One who cares for you.

_____

_____

_____

Trail Notes (questions, insights, prayers)

Susan R. Lawrence

Lace up your Hiking Boots

Stand firm then, with the belt of truth buckled around your waist, with the breastplate of righteousness in place, and with your feet fitted with the readiness that comes from the gospel of peace. (Ephesians 6:14-15)

"Hand me the moleskin, please," I requested.

On the fourth morning of a long section hike, my friend and I helped each other through our morning ritual—treating the blisters, sore toes, and tender areas of our feet. Uphill climbing rubbed blisters on our heels, descents jammed our feet into the toes of our boots, and the endless walking left tender spots between our toes. We cut pieces of the padded adhesive and made bandages, sticking them to our feet before we carefully eased our socks over them. Then we slipped our feet into our boots and laced them tightly.

Months before, we had thoughtfully chosen our footgear. We wore them several times, breaking them in and making sure there were no parts that rubbed. We thought we were ready. But our hiking boots could not protect us from the rigors of the trail. Eventually, our feet would toughen, our blisters would heal, and the morning ritual wouldn't be necessary. This morning, we needed the moleskin.

If you are a believer, you have the perfect hiking shoes for walking with Jesus. Ephesians 5 tells us to fit our feet into the gospel of peace. Our feet are our foundation; we can't walk without feet. The gospel is also our foundation. We can't be Christians without knowing who Jesus is, and what He accomplished for us.

It doesn't mean we won't occasionally get a blister or two when we walk with Jesus. Sometimes the way through the garden is a rock-strewn path. Let Jesus sit with you in the morning and apply bandages to the blisters. Eventually, you will find your feet growing tougher as they walk daily in the gospel that gives us the peace of knowing this walk is worth everything.

Conversing With My Guide
God, help me to stand and walk in the gospel of peace. Give me the strength to keep walking, even when it is difficult or painful.

Climb Higher
Ephesians 1-2

Stepping Out in Faith
As you put on your shoes for the day, take a minute to thank God for the gospel. Ask Him for power and readiness to walk in the gospel, and to share with others what God has accomplished.

Trail Notes (questions, insights, prayers)

Hiking Partners

He who walks with the wise grows wise, but a companion of fools suffers harm. (Proverbs 13:20)

A hiking companion should be chosen carefully. If you hike with me, you may spend the entire day, and maybe several days in a row, in the wilderness. You may or may not meet other people. I detest loud music on the trail, although loud laughter is great. I like to visit, except when I'm huffing and puffing on the steep inclines. But I'm okay with hiking in silence too. You must tolerate the antics of my young Lab as she is always with me. And you really need a sense of humor.

I have been blessed with several friends who are great companions. They not only tolerate all my quirks, but they also share my faith and a great love for God. We've been known to burst into songs of praise, or prayers for safety along the trail. Our conversations often inspire and encourage each other.

God does not intend for us to travel alone. He calls us to be in community and gives us the freedom to choose our close companions. Have you chosen people to surround you who will pray for you, encourage you, cheer you? Do those who walk with you build you up, or drag you down?

If your choice of companions is good, remember to express your gratitude. If you are hiking through life with fools, consider a change today.

Conversing With My Guide
Father, help me to choose my friends wisely. Thank you for the friends who support me, pray for me, and love me.

Climbing Higher
1 Corinthians 15:33
1 Thessalonians 5

Stepping Out in Faith
Call or write a personal note to someone who is a great companion on your path through life and thank them.

Trail Notes (questions, insights, prayers)
_____
_____
_____
_____
_____

Chiggers

In addition to all this, take up the shield of faith with which you can extinguish all the flaming arrows of the evil one. (Ephesians 6:16)

Do you have your camera? Sunglasses? Insect repellant? When preparing to step out on the trail, I like to think about the scenic views we will experience, the flowers that will color our path, or the wildlife we will spot. But I also need to prepare for some less delightful encounters. Mosquitoes, ticks, gnats, biting flies, bees, and chiggers love the woods as much as I do, and they are all eager to munch a lunch from my body. Chiggers, especially, seem to love my blood type. They burrow into places no insect should go and leave me scratching for weeks. So part of my routine is creating a shield of insect repellant over my boots, legs, and body. I don't want the memories of my day on the trail to be itchy welts.

God knows you will face assaults as you walk with Him. Jesus told his disciples (and us) *If they persecuted me, they will persecute you also.* (John 15:20b) Our persecution can take many forms. In the United States, Christians are rarely in bodily danger because of our faith. But hurtful comments, shunning, and attacks on our character are all possible and may be probable.

God wants you to be ready with the repellant. The shield of faith. It doesn't fire back; it just keeps the enemy's darts from harming us. The belief, or faith, that God is in control, God will have the ultimate victory, and nothing happens without His knowledge will shield us perfectly.

Conversing With My Guide
God, help me to hold what I know of You, my faith, as my shield against evil and those who would persecute me.

Climbing Higher
Hebrews 11-12

Stepping Out in Faith
Draw a shield and write on it a statement of what you know to be true of God. Hang it where it can serve as a reminder to you.

Trail Notes (questions, insights, prayers)

_____

_____

_____

_____

_____

Goals

So, we make it our goal to please Him, whether we are at home in the body or away from it. (2 Corinthians 5:9)

When I set out for a hike, I usually have a goal in mind. If I'm on the Appalachian Trail, a mountaintop is sure to be my destination. If I am on the Superior Trail, a waterfall or scenic overlook may be my goal. Sometimes my objective is to hike a certain number of miles, or to hike to a spot where my husband will pick me up. When I ride a favorite paved trail on my bike, my destination is the ice cream shop where I can relax in the gazebo and have a sweet treat.

A goal keeps me moving. When I stop for lunch, I take the map from my backpack and try to figure out how far I've come, how far I have to go, and how long it's going to take me. If I get weary, I think about that spectacular waterfall, or mountaintop, or even just the sight of my husband's red truck. Imagining my target helps me strap on my backpack and resume hiking.

When we walk with God, we need to have a goal, too. In 2 Corinthians 5:9 we find a simply stated purpose—we are to please Him. So, what pleases God? Surrender, obedience, the sacrifice of praise, the offering of love. We can start with those. Every day, in everything we do, we relentlessly push toward the goal of a life that pleases God.

Conversing With My Guide
God, help me see in my own life the areas I need to surrender to You, the ways I need to obey, the praises I need to offer, and the love I need to give. Let my goal be a life pleasing to You.

Climbing Higher
Philippians 3

Stepping Out in Faith
Write down one specific way you want to please God in surrender, obedience, praise or love.

_____

_____

_____

Trail Notes (questions, insights, prayers)

_____

_____

_____

Following the Leader

Dear children, do not let anyone lead you astray. He who does what is right is righteous, just as He is righteous. (1 John 3:7)

I hiked one portion of the Appalachian Trail (AT) with three friends. We took turns leading, being in the middle, and being last. Unfortunately, none of us had been gifted with a great sense of direction. There was often a collaboration of minds. Which way do we go? Is this the trail or a side trail?

One morning I led as we headed out. The previous evening, we had hiked into camp, so no shuttle was needed. We left from our campsite and walked down the intersecting trail. When we reached the Appalachian Trail, I turned away from the camp. The others hiked behind. We had gone quite a distance when we passed a signpost.

"I think we passed this yesterday," Leigh remarked.

I stopped and looked around. She was right. I'd turned in the wrong direction when we left camp, everyone had followed me, and we hiked a half mile the way we'd come the previous day. There was nothing to do but turn around, hike back to where we started, and then continue in that direction.

There will be others in your life who, intentionally or

mistakenly, try to lead you down the wrong path. Most often, it will not be someone who suggests criminal behavior, but someone who has inadvertently believed something that isn't true.

When my friends and I reached the intersection of the trail from camp and the AT, we should have paused, used the map or a compass, and determined the correct direction. But I just stepped out, believing I was headed the right way.

Before accepting as truth what you've read on the internet, or a friend has told you, use your compass—God's word, the Bible—to determine which way to go. Does it line up with what Scripture tells us? What does God say about the situation?

Conversing With My Guide
Heavenly Father, help me to follow only You. When others try to lead me in different directions help me to understand what Your Word says.

Climbing Higher
1 John 3
Galatians 1

Stepping Out in Faith
Make a list of things the world says that are not true, then cite by each a Bible verse that states God's truth.

Trail Notes (questions, insights, prayers)

Susan R. Lawrence

Blazes

Whether you turn to the right or to the left, your ears will hear a voice behind you saying, "This is the way; walk in it." (Isaiah 30:21)

Weariness slowed my walk. I felt like we'd been hiking for hours. Were we even on the right trail? I searched the woods ahead, but I couldn't see the white blaze that reassured me. Nothing to do but keep plodding forward. Then, like a light in the dark woods, I saw the familiar white rectangle. "I see a blaze!" I shouted to my hiking partners. Encouraged, we walked with lighter steps and hearts. We knew we were headed in the right direction.

Long-distance trails are usually marked. The most common mark is a blaze, a painted rectangle on a tree. The Appalachian Trail has white blazes, the Superior Trail has blue, and the Florida Trail has orange. The presence of more than one blaze on a tree is to alert you to a change in direction, an intersecting trail, or the trail's end. Sometimes, trails are marked with signposts that tell you how long the trail is, or if it's considered easy, moderate, or difficult. A kiosk at the trailhead may contain a map. These are all measures to keep you on the right track.

If I am slogging along, exhausted from climbing mountains, the sight of a blaze on a tree ahead of me never fails to cheer my heart.

It seems to say, "You're still on the trail, you're going in the right direction, you're not lost." If I hike with others, the lead person often shouts, "Blaze!" so we all see it and are uplifted.

In my walk with God, I often become weary. But He promises that we can know the way, we don't have to flounder around in the dark. I believe God creates *blazes* so we can know we are following the trail He has put us on.

First, we must step out. The promise in Isaiah is made to those who are walking. If you're feeling lost, you may need to just move forward in faith. Then search for the *blazes* God leaves for you. It may be a word of encouragement from a friend, a sermon, the lyrics in a song, or even that still small voice within that reminds you, "This is the way, walk in it."

Conversing With My Guide
Thank you, God, for the blazes you leave to guide us. Give us the strength to lift our heads and see them.

Climbing Higher
Exodus 13:17-22
Exodus 40:34-38

Stepping Out in Faith
Be someone's blaze today. Give a word of encouragement to a fellow walker—in person, through text, email, phone call, or a personal, written note.

Trail Notes (questions, insights, prayers)

Susan R. Lawrence

Boulders

Moses answered the people, "Do not be afraid. Stand firm and you will see the deliverance the Lord will bring you today...The Lord will fight for you; you need only to be still." (Exodus 14:13-14)

A frequent obstacle on almost any trail is a boulder. They come in all sizes. From small enough to step over and never break stride, to one I gaze up at thinking, "There is no way I'm going to get my body over that one." My short-legged, no-longer-young body can't always scramble over something easily. So I stand and survey the situation.

There may be a way around the boulder, like sidling on a narrow trail, or stepping into the woods. Or, if I look closely, I may be able to spot the footholds and protrusions others have used to climb up and over. Occasionally, I see a narrow slot, and I can literally step through the boulder.

We all have boulders in our lives. Those obstacles that bring us to a halt and, at first glance, make our way impossible. That was the situation the Israelites faced with the Red Sea before them and the Egyptian army hot on the trail behind them. And God told them, *You only need to be still.*

How impossible that seems in the face of boulders! I need to do something, I need to move the boulder out of my way, I need to attack the person who put this boulder in my path. Yet, God says, *be still.*

Only by being still and knowing God will fight for me, can I spot the path around the boulder, the way over the boulder, or even the way through the boulder.

Conversing With My Guide
Jesus, sometimes I face so many boulders. Thank you for walking with me. Help me to be still and let You show me the way forward.

Climbing Higher
Exodus 14
Psalm 46

Stepping Out in Faith
On a piece of paper write or draw a boulder or boulders you are facing. Now write across the paper, over what you have written, BE STILL. Practice that today.

Trail Notes (questions, insights, prayers)

_____

_____

_____

Look up!

I lift up my eyes to the hills—where does my help come from? My help comes from the Lord, Maker of heaven and earth. (Psalm 121:1-2)

When hiking a difficult trail—one strewn with rocks, roots or steep inclines—we tend to look at our feet, watching where we step so we don't trip. We focus only on the three feet of trail ahead of us. But we're missing the big picture. If we stop and look up, we may see some amazing scenery. It might be a breathtaking view, an interesting tree, or a busy squirrel or bird flitting through the bushes. So, I try to remind myself to stop every so often and lift my eyes to see what beauty God has provided.

In our day-to-day world, we can get caught up in the details of life instead of remembering the big picture. We worry about much that we can't control—health concerns, our children, situations at our workplace—life's issues can keep us awake. We're only looking at our feet. Lift up your eyes and see the One who is in charge. Our God, our Creator, has control. He may not allow us to see why this is happening, what will happen in the future, and how it will impact us—but we can lift our heads and focus on God. He loves us, He is in control, and He holds our future.

Susan R. Lawrence

Conversing With My Guide
God, help me to lift my head and look at the amazing picture of your grace for me. May I place the things that worry me in Your hands.

Climbing Higher
Psalm 121
Matthew 6:25-34

Stepping Out in Faith
Write down a list of things that you tend to worry about. By each one write, "Lift up your head—God's got this."

_____

_____

_____

Trail Notes (questions, insights, prayers)

_____

_____

_____

_____

_____

_____

Bridges

When you pass through the waters, I will be with you; and when you pass through the rivers, they will not sweep over you. (Isaiah 43:2)

I stood and looked at the bridge. The dirt below had heaved, the supports leaned at an angle, and the floor tilted precariously. Underneath, the river rushed and roiled. I did not want to do a water crossing. So, I stepped on the worn planks cautiously, easing one foot slowly after another. When my feet touched the earth on the other side, I rejoiced.

Most of the time, I love trail bridges. Whether they cross tiny streams that trickle by or large rivers, rushing and frothing, they are often the spot I choose for a break. Then I can stand and view the water. I have crossed well-built bridges with sturdy supports anchored deep and a rail to grasp. I have also crossed bridges that I wasn't sure would hold my weight, rotted structures with holes through which I could see far below. I chose to walk over all of them rather than be swept away in the water or risk getting my feet wet.

When walking with Jesus we will come to crossings as well, crossings that will take us to new places, new seasons of our life. We may hesitate, even cast a glance back the way we have come. The path we know may look easier, or safer. But Jesus is calling us to cross.

The passage from Isaiah reminds us He will be with us, and the waters won't sweep over us. Jesus will build a bridge for our crossing. It may look a bit dangerous, we may see the water through the holes, but Jesus is leading.

If you face a crossing on a path to which God has called you, don't hesitate, step out in faith. On the other side, you will rejoice.

Conversing With My Guide
God, give me the courage to face my crossings boldly, knowing You walk beside me and protect me.

Climbing Higher
Isaiah 43

Stepping Out in Faith
Find or draw a picture of a bridge. Add the caption, *When you pass through the waters, I will be with You, Jesus.*

Trail Notes (questions, insights, prayers)

_____

_____

_____

_____

_____

Level Ground

Teach me to do your will, for You are my God; may Your good Spirit lead me on level ground. (Psalm 143:10)

My hiking partners and I stumbled at last to the summit. But instead of a round rock top, a long ridge stretched in front of us. The deep forest had thinned, and sunlight dappled everything. Beside us, lacey ferns waved and stretched as far as we could see. A soft layer of pine needles covered the path. We no longer struggled to breathe or had concerns about slipping or tripping. We could view the fern meadow without hinderance.

However, the long, gentle walk did not build up our muscles, increase our lung capacity, force our hearts to work harder, or even give us that great feeling of accomplishment from having climbed a mountain. The ridgetop refreshed us, but our bodies didn't gain the benefits of the uphill climbs.

Whether hiking in the mountains or through life, we need both level walks and mountain climbs. James 1:2 convicts me every time I read it. *Count it all joy, my brothers, whenever you face trials of many kinds, because you know that the testing of your faith develops perseverance.*

Enduring our trials is like climbing mountains. We slip and trip. We struggle to breathe. We cannot see our surroundings because we are so focused on what is right in front of us—the looming rock. But James says to count it joy. Because climbing the mountain builds spiritual muscle. It increases our heart capacity. And we breathe the breath of the Spirit. We need to shout praises from the valley all the way to the mountain top.

Conversing With My Guide
God, thank You for the ridgetops in my walk—the times I feel so grand, I can sail through anything. Thank You, too, for the mountains, when I struggle along. Because I know that, through the struggle, I will be stronger and more able to persevere.

Climbing Higher
2 Peter 1

Stepping Out in Faith
Find a hill to walk up today. As you go, name the mountains God has allowed in your life and thank Him for them.

Trail Notes (questions, insights, prayers)

_____

_____

_____

_____

Shell Collections

Do not store up for yourselves treasures on earth, where moth and rust destroy, and where thieves break in and steal. But store up for yourselves treasures in heaven, where moth and rust do not destroy, and where thieves do not break in and steal. For where your treasure is, there your heart will be also. (Matthew 6:19-21)

One of my favorite places to hike is a beach. The wide flat stretches of sand are amazing to walk on, and I have an endless scenic view. But I often miss the panorama due to my fascination with shells. When I'm on a beach my head is usually down, searching for the largest, most beautiful, most unique shells to add to my collection. If I spot one and pick it up, I turn it over in my hands, looking for defects, and if it passes inspection, I put it in my bag, then begin searching for the next treasure. I can spend hours on the beach and rarely look up from the sand.

When I finally lift my head, I can see what I've ignored. The breathtaking, awesome view of the ocean—the never-ending folding and unfolding of the waves, the changing colors—white on the crest, blues and greens in all shades, and the dark depths below.

The last time I walked on a beach there were windsurfers, looking like gigantic butterflies perched on the ocean. Their grace and skill mesmerized me for several minutes. There are always birds swooping in and out, foraging on the beach, or floating peacefully between waves.

Are you walking through life focused on the sand and what you can accumulate? The mundane tasks of life, or earthly treasures, can drain us quickly if we do not take time to look up at the ocean of God's love, goodness, and grace. Lift your head from the sand, fill your heart with treasure from Heaven, and give thanks.

Conversing With My Guide
Father, forgive me for wrong priorities, for concentrating on accumulating treasures on earth rather than filling myself with your oceans of blessings.

Climbing Higher
Matthew 6

Stepping Out in Faith
Do something today that stores up treasures in Heaven. Connect with someone you haven't seen for a while, do a good deed for someone in need, or spend extra time with family.

Trail Notes (questions, insights, prayers)

_____

_____

_____

Lost

Trust in the Lord with all your heart and lean not on your own understanding. In all your ways acknowledge Him and He will direct your paths. (Proverbs 3:5-6)

I'm thankful I've never been totally lost, but I have had moments when I wasn't sure where the trail was. Other times, an unmarked intersection forced a choice—one way correct, the other not—or there could be a temporary split in the trail, and either way is correct, but I couldn't see it from where I stood.

My friend, Angela, and I emerged from the trail onto Skyline Drive. We took a minute or two to get a drink and then crossed the road. Most of the Appalachian Trail we'd followed thus far was well-marked. But now, we saw no signage, and no trail. We couldn't just stand on the road and fret, so we walked a short distance up a driveway to find it was clearly marked "Private Drive, no trespassing."

We consulted our maps, which plainly showed the trail crossing the road. We crisscrossed Skyline Drive two or three times searching for the start of the trail on the other side. Finally, we located the sign, hidden from view in the trees, in the opposite direction of the driveway. With great sighs of relief, we headed down the path.

Often, I'm unsure of the path I am to take in life. I pour out my heart to God, pleading for direction, and there is no answer.

What should I do?

    Sometimes, when there is no obvious answer, God simply waits for you to draw near to Him believing your circumstances will work for your good, and that He is already directing your paths. Stop fretting, take the next step, and trust the One who leads.

Conversing With My Guide
Father in Heaven, let me trust in You always. Thank you for directing my paths, for being faithful. Amen

Climbing Higher
Jeremiah 10:23-24
Psalm 56:3-4
John 14

Stepping Out in Faith
Find or draw a picture of a road, path, or trail. Print it and title it, *God directs my paths*. Put it where you will see it frequently.

Trail Notes (questions, insights, prayers)

_____

_____

_____

_____

Reflections

And we, who with unveiled faces all reflect the Lord's glory, are being transformed into his likeness with ever-increasing glory, which comes from the Lord, who is the Spirit. (2 Corinthians 3:18)

My husband and I camped in Chequamegon National Forest several times as leaves changed in late September or early October. We chose campsites near tiny Lake Wanoka, nestled amid the trees. In the fall, the ring of trees takes on spectacular colors. The reds and yellows of the maples contrast with taller, deep-green pine spires. When the sun rises or sets, this colorful show is reflected perfectly in the calm waters of the lake. The breath-taking view is one that never fails to call me to worship and praise God.

For Lake Wanoka to have those lovely reflections, the sun must be shining on it.

For us to reflect God's glory, His Son must shine through us. When we know Jesus and believe in Him as our Savior, God gives us the gift of His Holy Spirit who lives within.

For Lake Wanoka to show perfect reflections, the water needs to be calm and still.

For us to show God's glory, our spirit needs to be calm. Let the One who stills the wind and waves calm your spirit.

When we camped at Chequamegon, there were only a few other campers, and they weren't at the lake. So my husband and I alone inhaled the beauty of the reflections.

Your reflection may shine on a single person or on a great crowd. God will choose the people in your life on whom He wants to reflect His glory. We need to shine for whoever God sends.

How well are you reflecting today?

Conversing With My Guide
God, help me to be the best reflection of Your glory that I can. Help me to believe without wavering. Calm the tumult and storms within me. Let me reflect Your glory to all those I meet.

Climbing Higher
Psalm 67

Stepping Out in Faith
Write down the names of one or more people for whom you want reflect God's love. Then make a plan to do it.

_____

_____

_____

_____

_____

Trail Notes (questions, insights, prayers)

Susan R. Lawrence

Snake!

Be self-controlled and alert. Your enemy the devil prowls around like a roaring lion looking for someone to devour. (1 Peter 5:8)

The summer sun shone gently through the trees, the quiet woods lay as far as we could see, and the great Mississippi River flowed below us. Two friends and I were trekking in a State Forest in Northeast Iowa, and the day was perfect. I led as the trail wound gently up and down, but nothing too strenuous. We were making good time and intended to spend the day in this portion of the forest. We all stopped for a drink and switched positions.

Leigh, who preferred a brisk pace, chuckled, "I guess if I'm leading, I need to watch further ahead than my own feet." We chatted as we walked, the casual conversations of good friends, following the trail as it curved away from the river.

Suddenly, Leigh stopped. She took a few steps back and pointed—a huge snake, well-camouflaged in the leaves, curled up on the trail directly in front of us. I used the leash to pull my inquisitive pup close to my side. Both Gwen and Leigh took photos of him, and Gwen used her phone to identify him as a timber rattler.

We were unsure what to do. He looked like he was sleeping,

but we wanted him to move off the trail. One of us threw a tiny stick, hoping to startle him into moving away. Instead, he raised his tail and shook his rattle.

We backed up, plotted a way through the woods around where he lay, and took the detour. Then we continued hiking, but all three of us were definitely *rattled*. So, we shortened our hike and ate our lunch in a park where the grass was mowed, and nothing lurked in hiding.

The Bible calls the devil *our enemy, the serpent,* and a *roaring lion*. We were so grateful that Leigh was *self-controlled and alert*. She spotted the snake in time so we could move off the path and avoid him.

The devil is as real as that timber rattler was. But he won't saunter down your path of life and politely introduce himself. Like the rattler, he is well camouflaged. He may hide in social media, news reports, ads, even in our church work and ministries.

The devil's purpose is to interrupt and even end your walk with God. We need to stay alert, make positive identification, and take a detour.

Conversing with my Guide
God, help me be wise when I spot the devil trying to interrupt our relationship. Give me courage and strength to identify and resist him every time.

Climbing Higher
1 Peter 5
Ephesians 4:27
James 4:7

Stepping out in Faith

Write down areas in which you struggle. Make a plan to resist the devil in each situation.

Susan R. Lawrence

Trail Notes (questions, insights, prayers)

Teepees and Rock Cairns

...the Lord said to Joshua, "Choose twelve men from among the people, one from each tribe, and tell them to take up twelve stones from the middle of the Jordan from right where the priests stood and carry them over with you and put them down at the place where you stay tonight." (Joshua 4:1-3)

Although we all object to those who leave trash on a trail, hikers differ in their opinions regarding teepees and rock cairns. The history of cairns stretches back to ancient times when travelers used them for markers on roads and trails. They are still used for that purpose on some trails, especially in desert or rocky areas where a path is not clearly visible.

In current times, people often build them for fun. Adding a small rock to an existing sculpture appeals to our creative urge and connects you to people who have gone that way before. Crawling into a structure built of downed branches makes you feel like you are adventuring not just down a trail, but back in time to when people built similar teepees for shelter. Please be aware some places, including National Parks, prohibit movement of rocks and downed wood, so know the rules before you go.

God commanded the Israelites to leave stones as markers—altars for worship, but also to commemorate events in their history for future generations.

"...when your children ask you, 'What do these stones mean?' tell them that the flow of the Jordan was cut off before the ark of the covenant of the Lord. When it crossed the Jordan, the waters of the Jordan were cut off. These stones are to be a memorial to the people of Israel forever." (Joshua 4:6-7)

Far more important to me than leaving a rock on a pile is to be used by God to build His Kingdom. What in my life is going to make others ask, "What does this mean?" What can I display as a personal reminder of great things God has done for me?

Conversing With My Guide
Almighty Father, thank you for all the ways you have shown me your loving kindness. Let me not take this for granted. But soften my heart to share with others the love You have showered on me.

Climbing Higher
Joshua 4

Stepping Out in Faith
In your home or workplace, display something to remind you of times when God's loving kindness has been evident in your life.

Trail Notes (questions, insights, prayers)

_____

_____

He Walks With Me

Susan R. Lawrence

Mary's Rock

Hear my cry, O God, listen to my prayer. From the ends of the earth I call to you, I call as my heart grows faint; Lead me to the rock that is higher than I. (Psalm 61:1-2)

My legs burned and my lungs struggled for air. We were hiking a two-week section of the Appalachian Trail and this narrow, rocky path rose straight up. This was not a part of the main trail, but we had seen the sign for *Mary's Rock* and were intrigued. The arrow pointed up an incline and stated that it was only one mile. Energized by our good night's sleep in the camping trailer and a hearty breakfast, my friend agreed—we should do this. So, we climbed and climbed and climbed. Sweating and puffing, we labored upwards. It seemed we would never reach the top. I looked at Leigh, and gasped, "Do you want to turn back?" Leigh stood up straight, shook her head emphatically and continued climbing.

We skirted a large boulder—and suddenly we stood on top of the world. Below us, hazy blue and green mountains undulated until they scraped the sky. For several minutes, we remained frozen, taking in the breathtaking view, and knowing the two miles added to our day's trail had been totally worth it. We drank in the scenery, took pictures, and rested. We knew we still had a long day of hiking ahead, but we were reluctant to leave.

Jesus is the rock that is higher than I, the solid rock, our firm foundation. Sometimes, as we trudge through this life, sweating and puffing, we wonder if it's worth it. Life seems to be one boulder after another. We may even hear someone whisper, "Just quit."

But when we stand on the mountain top with Him, we know without a doubt He is worth the climb. Standing face to face with Jesus will be far more breathtaking than the beauty of Mary's Rock. So, when you encounter the next boulder or rocky trail in this life, hold tight to His hand and keep your eye on the prize. The end of the trail will be the best view you've ever seen.

Conversing With My Guide
God, give me the strength to keep climbing through this life. Thank you for sending Jesus, who died that I might live and someday stand on the mountaintop with You.

Climbing Higher
2 Timothy 2-4

Stepping Out in Faith
Write down a "boulder" you are facing today. Talk to God about it and ask Him to give you strength to deal with it.

Trail Notes (questions, insights, prayers)

_____

_____

_____

Snacks

Even youths grow tired and weary, and young men stumble and fall; but those who hope in the Lord will renew their strength. They will soar on wings like eagles; they will walk and not be faint. (Isaiah 40:30-31)

Hiking, especially in rough terrain, takes a lot of energy. So, when I go for an all-day hike, I take a few snacks in addition to my lunch. When anyone needs a break, we stop.

The lunch stop consists of finding the right place to sit comfortably (as comfortable as a fallen tree or flat rock can be,) removing backpacks, drinking, eating, and resting. A snack is a shorter affair. Sometimes it's just some crackers and cheese or beef sticks leftover from lunch. Sometimes it's a granola bar, maybe even one with enough chocolate to qualify as a dessert. Whatever we pull out of our backpack gives us energy and refreshes us to begin hiking again.

God, Jehovah Jireh, our Provider, nourishes us in every way. He provides food for our physical requirements. He provides hiking for our mental refreshment. (It works for me!) And He provides His Word for our spiritual need. We must regularly feast on His word, but sometimes even daily reading is not enough. We need some snacks.

Snacking on God's word might mean remembering verses you have memorized. It could be listening to Christian music, or a phone call with a friend who will pray with you or share a Bible verse. It might be reading a page of a devotional such as this. It could even be opening a Bible app on your phone rather than social media.

When you are dashing about, checking off the items of your busy life, be sure to stop regularly for a God snack. You will be given energy and refreshment to continue.

Conversing With My Guide
God, forgive me for the times I get so busy that I forget to let You nourish me with Your Word. Help me to remember who You are—my God who provides.

Climbing Higher
Psalm 119

Stepping Out in Faith
Organize your life so that God snacks are handy. Program your radio to a Christian station or bookmark Christian songs on your app. Leave your Bible and devotionals in a convenient place for quick reading. Put a Bible reading app on your phone for all those times you must wait.

Trail Notes (questions, insights, prayers)

Susan R. Lawrence

Here's a Red Carpet for You

God saw all that He had made, and it was very good.
(Genesis 1:31)

Angela, Leigh, and I had been hiking the Superior Trail for several days. The rugged terrain and long days meant aching bodies and weary muscles. But we had worked our way north, and the woods had begun to sport fall colors. We walked in silence, occasionally pointing out a particularly splendid tree.

I turned a corner into a stand of red maples. As far as I could see, the trail was covered with bright crimson leaves. Awestruck, I stopped and took in the view as my hiking partners came up beside me.

"God's spread out the red carpet for us," I remarked. Then we resumed our hike, reveling in the beautiful view, and the reminder of God's love for us.

God has indeed spread a red carpet for us. His invitation to spend eternity in Heaven with Him comes through Jesus Christ, who died on the cross to pay for our sins. We walk into Heaven on the red carpet of Jesus's blood.

There is much that is wrong with our world. Since man first sinned, the consequences have reached every little corner. Yet, there is also much that is breathtaking. From the delicate beauty of the tiniest wildflower, to the towering trees of the northern forests, to the spectacular views of rugged canyons—our world is filled with beauty, created by God, for us. This is where He chose to place you and me. Every time God amazes you with something beautiful, remind yourself that God has rolled out the red carpet of His creation as a reminder of His love, His sending-his-only-Son love, for you.

Conversing With My Guide
Almighty God, thank you for the beauty of the earth that we call home. Help me to see its beauty in what You have created and know the depth of Your love.

Climbing Higher
John 3:16
Ecclesiastes 3:11
Job 38-39

Stepping Out in Faith
Find a flower, a tree branch, a rock—something to remind you of the Creator. Thank Him for His great love.

Trail Notes (questions, insights, prayers)

_____

_____

_____

The Map

Your word is a lamp to my feet and a light for my path. (Psalm 119:105)

"They're here!" I shouted to my husband as I hurried into the house, clutching a package I'd ordered from Amazon. I sliced it open and spilled the contents onto the table—a book, *Appalachian Trail Guide to Shenandoah National Park,* and three packages of maps of the sections I intended to hike. For the next several weeks, I poured over the maps, planning the section we would hike each day of the two weeks on the trail. I noted distances, possible obstacles, and drop-off and pick-up locations for my husband, who was our shuttle driver.

When we began the actual hiking, I placed the map of that section in the pocket of my backpack. Several times a day, one of us would say, "Let's get the map out." We needed it for clarification on how far we'd come, what we might encounter next, and where we could locate water. Without the trail guide and the maps, it would be like trying to navigate a trail without sight.

When we walk with God, He doesn't want us wandering around without a clue where we're going. So, He gave us His Word, the Bible, the only perfect map for Christian living.

How foolish it would have been for me to start on the trail

without a map! And how foolish it is for us to try to navigate life's paths without His map for us.

As you walk on life's journey, be quick to say in every situation, "Let's get the map out. What does the Bible say?" It contains everything you need to know about any trail God leads you on.

Conversing With My Guide
God, kindle in me a deep desire to study and follow your map. Keep me in the Word, every day, in every situation.

Climbing Higher
Psalm 1

Stepping Out in Faith
Make a plan to increase or be more consistent in your daily intake of Scripture.

Trail Notes (questions, insights, prayers)
_____
_____
_____
_____
_____

The Good Way

This is what the Lord says, "Stand at the crossroads and look, ask for the ancient paths, ask where the good way is, and walk in it, and you will find rest for your souls." (Jeremiah 6:16)

A trail map is essential. A guidebook, compass, blaze, and trail signage are all useful too. But nothing is more helpful than someone who has already traveled the trail. I belong to several Facebook groups for hikers. If you're planning a hike in the future, you can receive valuable information on parking at the trailhead, favorite portions of a trail, difficulty level, water availability, and things to look out for. But nothing replaces personal face-to-face testimony. "Is this the trail to___?" "How much further?" "Is there water ahead?"

The first time I climbed Blood Mountain in Georgia, I had no idea what I was in for. About three-fourths of the way up, I stopped and sat on a rock to catch my breath. A group of hikers stepped around the corner on their way down. I gasped out, "Is it much further to the top?"

"No, you're almost there," they encouraged me. Refreshed and heartened by their words, I resumed my climb and in a short time reached the summit.

God did not intend that we walk a solitary path through life.

He placed us with others so we could support one another. Someone you know is climbing a mountain today and can't see the summit. You can be the guide who shows them the way, or the cheerleader who encourages them to finish. Who does God want you to guide or be a cheerleader for today?

Conversing With My Guide
God, thank you for those in my life who have encouraged me in my walk with you. Help me to be a guide and an encourager to those you put on my path.

Climbing Higher
2 Timothy 4:1-2
Hebrews 3:13
Hebrews 10:19-39

Stepping Out in Faith
Write two notes—one thanking someone for encouraging you, and one to someone who needs to be encouraged.

Trail Notes (questions, insights, prayers)

_____

_____

_____

_____

No Need for Headlamps

Come, O house of Jacob, let us walk in the light of the Lord. (Isaiah 2:5)

One thing I aways carry in my backpack is a light. I would never intentionally hike in the dark, but sometimes accidents happen—you lose your way, someone is injured, or the difficulty of the trail slows you down. So, I am prepared. When we planned a hike in November, my husband—who doesn't hike with me but always cares for me—ordered two headlamps, one for me and one for my hiking partner. He knew the daylight hours were shorter that time of year, and we had never hiked this particular trail before, so he wanted us to be prepared. I'm thankful I have never needed that headlamp, but I still carry it.

God doesn't want us hiking in the dark either. He sent His Son to be our light. Jesus told His disciples (and us) *"I am the Light of the world."* (John 8:12)

What do we need to do to ensure we are not walking in darkness?

1. Spend time in God's word. *Your word is...a light for my path.* (Psalm 119:105)
2. Love one another. *Anyone who claims to be in the light but hates his brother is still in the darkness.* (1 John 2:9)
3. Refrain from deliberate sin. *If we claim to have fellowship with*

him yet walk in the darkness, we lie and do not live by the truth. (1 John 1:6)
4. Let others see Jesus in you. *In the same way, let your light shine before men, that they may see your good deeds and praise your Father in Heaven. (Matthew 5:16)*

When we do these things consistently, we won't hike in darkness, no matter what circumstances surround us.

Conversing With My Guide
Jesus, let me walk with You in the light. Help me resist the darkness and crave Your holy light.

Climbing Higher
1 John 2

Stepping Out in Faith
Light a candle, lamp, or other source of light that is usually not lit. Every time you see it, thank God for giving us Jesus, and ask Him to shine His light through you.

Trail Notes (questions, insights, prayers)

_____

_____

_____

Toe Jam

Consider it pure joy, my brothers, whenever you face trials of many kinds, because you know that the testing of your faith develops perseverance. (James 1:2-3)

Let's talk about toe jam—and I don't mean the fuzzy stuff that accumulates between your toes. When I am climbing a steep ascent, I huff and puff and struggle, trying to get air into my lungs. My legs throb from the exertion. My back aches as my pack gets heavier and heavier. I think, *If I can just get to the top, things will be easier.*

After reaching the mountain top, I take a few minutes to admire the view, let my breathing slow to a normal rate, and get a drink. Then I start to descend the other side. And the toe jam begins. If the way is steep, each step jams my feet into the toe of my hiking shoes. The pain on tender toes is excruciating.

The descent I thought would bring some relief just adds discomfort in a different area. So why do I continue doing something that causes me physical pain? Because, to me, it is worth any discomfort to walk in quiet solitude, surrounded by wilderness, and to stand on the mountain top. Then when I finish the hike and accomplish my goal, the pain is forgotten.

Isn't life like that? We are going through a difficult time, and we look ahead to the next season of life to bring relief. *It will be better when the kids are grown. It will be better in my new job. It will be better if we make this move. It will be better when we have more money.*

But when that new season comes, we have pain in a different area. Jesus told us, *In this world you will have trouble.* (John 16:33) There is no one who will disagree with that.

James tells us to *consider it pure joy!* That may seem impossible, but we can manage it if we keep our eyes on the goal. Our hike through this world is temporary. And so is the pain. Count it joy whether you go up the mountain or down, he leads you. And he has promised, *But, take heart! I have overcome the world.* (John 16:33)

Conversing With My Guide
Father, it is so hard to find joy in the seasons of pain. Remind me of this world's impermanence. And lift my soul today.

Climbing Higher
James 1

Stepping Out in Faith
Do something to uplift your soul today. Go for a walk, sing a praise song, or write a prayer of gratitude.

Trail Notes (questions, insights, prayers)

_____

_____

_____

What Do You See?

Finally, brothers, whatever is true, whatever is noble, whatever is right, whatever is pure, whatever is lovely, whatever is admirable—if anything is excellent or praiseworthy—think about such things. (Philippians 4:8)

I rarely walk without finding numerous treasures. If there are wildflowers blooming, I stop for a picture. If a bird has dropped a feather, I pick it up and try to identify what species it came from. If there is an unusual rock, it usually ends up in my pocket. Trees often catch my eye—a dead one with bare branches reaching to the sky, a lone one in a field with lush foliage, a fallen one with a heart-shaped hollow center. One friend told me I have "hunter's eyes." Other hiking partners get frustrated by my frequent stops and picture-taking. I enjoy the journey and find beauty in every corner of creation.

As I was pondering this facet of my personality, I asked God, "Why do I spot things on the trail that others seem to miss?"

The answer popped into my mind. *I want you to see people the way you see items on a trail.* This thought stopped me in my tracks.

How many of God's people-creations do I tend to criticize rather than praise? I see what they are doing that I consider wrong, and I think it needs to be addressed. Maybe I need to see the heart-shaped, hollow center of the person and see how beautiful they are.

I love even the tattered and spent wildflower. Do I love the tattered and spent person I meet on the street?

I keep the odd or unusual rocks that I find. Do I treasure the odd and unusual people who cross my path?

If we begin to see people the way God sees them, we will begin to love as He does. And not only do we have the power to transform their lives, it can transform ours as well.

Conversing With My Guide
God, help me to see your beauty in all your creation—including people. Help me see everyone with Your eyes and love them with Your heart.

Climbing Higher
Genesis 1

Stepping Out in Faith
Write a list of those people you are tempted to criticize. Find something beautiful in them instead, thank God for them, and tell the person what you appreciate about them.

Trail Notes (questions, insights, prayers)

_____

_____

_____

_____

Sticktights

But the fruit of the Spirit is love, joy, peace, patience, kindness, goodness, faithfulness, gentleness, and self-control. Against such things there is no law. (Galatians 5:22)

One sunny fall day we hiked near home on the wide gravel paths that wound through the Red Feather Prairie. When we reached the paved bicycle path, I suggested we turn off the main trail onto a lesser-used foot path to Saylorville Reservoir. My hiking buddies agreed, especially my Labrador pup, Maggie.

We followed the dog's lead, weaving between the underbrush, stepping over fallen trees, and even going off the path to bypass a large limb that blocked our way. Eventually we stepped out from the trees to a wonderful view of the lake stretching for miles in either direction. We gazed at the geese, herons, and sea gulls feeding near the shore.

Then we looked at our clothing. All of us, including the pup, were covered with burrs—the kind I referred to as *sticktights*. Meaning you couldn't simply brush them off. We would have to spend hours picking the seeds individually from our clothes.

With a sigh, I sat on the log facing the lake and began the

tedious task of removal. Clearly, I had not chosen the best trail.

Some trails through life take us through *sticktights*. Certain shows we watch on TV, or books we read, or places we frequent, may cause words to stick in our vocabulary or leave images in our minds. Being around some people can encourage bitterness, anger, or gossip to reside in us. Just like the burrs on our clothes, the language or attitudes stick tight and are visible to others. Once stuck in our thought patterns, removing language, images, or attitudes can be a lengthy and difficult process.

Conversely, spending time with Jesus in prayer or in His Word can inspire love, joy, peace, patience, kindness, goodness, faithfulness, gentleness, and self-control to be the attitudes that stick tight to us.

Choose your trails carefully, so others will see the right sticktights in you.

Conversing With My Guide
Father, help me to always walk with you. Let Your paths be the ones I choose, and Your Holy Spirit's fruit the sticktights on me.

Climbing Higher
Galatians 5-6

Stepping Out in Faith
Choose one fruit of the Spirit to concentrate on. Consciously try to exhibit that fruit throughout the day.

Trail Notes (questions, insights, prayers)

Susan R. Lawrence

Weak Knees

Therefore, strengthen your feeble arms and weak knees.
(Hebrews 12:12)

Knees are important in hiking, and feeble arms won't pull you up the next rock scramble. So, I do what I can to strengthen my body. I do stretching and balancing exercises in the morning. I try to keep my weight to a healthy level. I exercise often—walking, biking, and doing garden and outdoor work.

When I get weary while hiking, I know that I need to stop, get a drink, rest, and maybe eat something. Then my body is strengthened, and I can continue.

The writer of Hebrews isn't referring to our physical knees. This verse comes midway between an exhortation to refrain from sin and endure hardship as discipline, and a section endorsing righteous living and a warning against refusing God. So, this refers to our spiritual knees. Sometimes, they need to be strengthened as well. Spiritual knees gain strength when we're on our physical knees in prayer.

We can resist sin and endure hardships by faithful, fervent prayer. Being honest and pouring out our hearts to God keeps us in a right relationship with Him and fortifies us to walk the paths God gives us.

Conversing With My Guide
Lord, help me to be diligent in my prayer life. I want to have strong spiritual knees and a right relationship with you.

Climbing Higher
James 5
Isaiah 35

Stepping Out in Faith
Spend some additional time today in prayer. If you do physical exercises, use that time for prayer to strengthen your spiritual knees as well as your physical ones.

Trail Notes (questions, insights, prayers)
_____
_____
_____
_____
_____
_____

He Walks With Me

What Trips You?

Therefore, since we are surrounded by such a great cloud of witnesses, let us throw off everything that hinders and the sin that so easily entangles, and let us run with perseverance the race marked out for us. (Hebrews 12:1)

"Ooops!" Leigh stumbled and almost fell on the narrow trail. I watched my steps closely and stepped over the tree roots hidden by fallen leaves. We were hiking the Superior Trail in northern Minnesota, and this day's section held hundreds of intertwining roots from the towering trees. Avoiding the roots proved impossible, and we did our best to step over or on them, so we didn't trip. Some segments held so many we needed to step from root to root, our feet aching from balancing on their hard, rounded surfaces.

The Superior Trail Race takes place on this trail. Participants run over the rocky and root-covered sections of trail we now labored slowly along. We marveled at their abilities as we minced our way, trying to navigate the roots.

In your walk with God, what trips you up? If you can, make a path around it. But avoiding sin can be as impossible as avoiding the roots we encountered. Sometimes we know exactly what will trip us, but the situation cannot be circumvented. If I am angry, I can be unkind. If someone has hurt me, I have trouble forgiving. I can't avoid all situations that may cause anger or hurt. But I can control my response to them. We need to slow down and step over the sin, and not let it trip us.

Of course, we know that if we do stumble and fall, we can stand up, brush ourselves off by asking forgiveness, and continue our walk. *If we confess our sins, He is faithful and just and will forgive us our sins and purify us from all unrighteousness.* (1 John 1:9)

Perhaps someday I will be able to race along life's trail, but for now I go slowly, watching for what might trip me, trying to avoid it, stepping over it, and asking for forgiveness when I fall.

Conversing With My Guide
Heavenly Father, be my strength as I seek to avoid the sins that entangle me. Forgive me when I do fall.

Climbing Higher
Psalm 51

Stepping Out in Faith
For what sins do you need to ask forgiveness today? Spend time with the Father in confession and bathe in His incredible grace.

Trail Notes (questions, insights, prayers)

He Walks With Me

Susan R. Lawrence

The Way Everlasting

See if there is any offensive way in me, and lead me in the way everlasting. (Psalm 139:24)

Why do I love hiking? I love being outside, especially in a forest. I love exercise, time with friends, or time alone. I love exploring new areas, seeing magnificent vistas or tiny wildflowers almost hidden in the leaves. Hiking refreshes me—physically, mentally, and spiritually. As I hike, I sometimes wonder what the scenery in Heaven will be like. Will there be mountains, pine-covered footpaths, rushing streams, or gorgeous fall colors? It won't matter because of the One I will be with.

Because I chose to give my life to Jesus as a small child and reaffirmed that decision as a young adult, I walk with Jesus.

He has promised never to leave me or forsake me. Deuteronomy 31:6

He will light every path I take. John 8:12

He died to give me the opportunity walk with Him. Colossians 1:19-20

He has shown me the way. John 14:6

My faith in Jesus Christ alone leads me in the way everlasting—the way to Heaven. And nothing in this world is more important than that.

So, dear friends, get outside and walk as often as you can. But always, walk with the One who loves you best, and the One who will lead you into everlasting life with Him.

Conversing With My Guide
God, Thank You for Your gift of eternal life through Jesus Christ Your Son. May I never take that for granted.

Climbing Higher
Deuteronomy 31:6
John 8:12
Colossians 1:19-20
John 14:6
John 3:16

Stepping Out in Faith
Write your own prayer, thanking Jesus for always walking through life with you.

Trail Notes (questions, insights, prayers)

_____

_____

_____

_____

The Delight of a Firm Foundation

He lifted me out of the slimy pit, out of the mud and mire; he set my feet on a rock and gave me a firm place to stand. (Psalm 40:2)

Many mountains have on or near the summit, large flat rocks with spectacular views. After climbing for a long time, reaching one of these places is a relief. I usually take the opportunity to unstrap my backpack, sit down, and rest. If it is close to lunchtime, I pull out my food and eat, enjoying the scenery. I stretch out my legs, and sometimes even fully recline, using my backpack as a pillow. After scrambling over small rocks and larger boulders on the trail, the smooth surface feels wonderful and is always a cause for celebration.

When we first accept Jesus Christ as our Savior, He pulls us out of the slimy pit of sin, and gives us the gift of eternal life with God—a very firm place to stand indeed. But sometimes, we don't act like we have a firm foundation. Instead, we behave as if we're still floundering in the slimy pit of sin or still climbing around boulders.

I believe God wants us to know we are on a firm place, and act accordingly. Rejoice. Unstrap your backpack, recline, and enjoy the view before you.

Your salvation, purchased by Jesus on the cross, is the

foundation for your entire life. Show the world that you stand on the flattest, smoothest rock there is.

Conversing With My Guide
Jesus, thank You for pulling me out of sin and into a new life with You. Help me to live each day with that truth as my foundation.

Climbing Higher
2 Timothy 2

Stepping Out in Faith
Find a smooth rock, write on it with a permanent marker, *He set my feet on a rock.* Place it where it can remind you of your salvation.

Trail Notes (questions, insights, prayers)

_____

_____

_____

_____

_____

_____

TO MY READERS: I pray that *He Walks With Me* has blessed, encouraged, and perhaps led you closer to the One who guides us on all our paths.

Your purchase of this book blesses others as well. All proceeds go to Pour International to maintain homes for abandoned babies and children in eSwatini, Africa. For more information on this organization, please go to www.info@pourinternational.org.

Other books by Susan R. Lawrence:

Atonement for Emily Adams
The Blue Marble
The Long Ride Home
Shepherd of eSwatini
Restoration at River's Edge
Flight of the Red-Winged Blackbird
Three Dogs' Tales

I love to connect with readers at www.susanrlawrence.com

Also published by Gannah Group Publications

Fiction by Susan R. Lawrence:
    Restoration at River's Edge

Speculative fiction series by Yvonne Anderson:
    Gateway to Gannah
        Story in the Stars
        Words in the Wind
        Ransom in the Rock
        The Last Toqeph
    The Four Lives of J. S. Freeman
        Stillwater
        Citizen
        Free

Nonfiction by Edith Harrington
    Dancing on Stones: A Quest for Joy